KAREN LATCHANA KENNEY

THE SCIENCE OF ROLLER COASTERS

UNDERSTANDING ENERGY

Checkerboard Library

An Imprint of Abdo Publishing
abdopublishing.com

abdopublishing.com

Published by Abdo Publishing, a division of ABDO, PO Box 398166, Minneapolis, Minnesota 55439. Copyright © 2016 by Abdo Consulting Group, Inc. International copyrights reserved in all countries. No part of this book may be reproduced in any form without written permission from the publisher. Checkerboard Library™ is a trademark and logo of Abdo Publishing.

Printed in the United States of America, North Mankato, Minnesota

102015
012016

Design: Christa Schneider
Production: Mighty Media, Inc.
Editor: Rebecca Felix

Cover Photos: Shutterstock, front cover, back cover
Interior Photos: AP Images, p. 14; Getty Images, p. 17; iStockphoto, pp. 21, 22, 23, 25, 27; Mighty Media, Inc., pp. 4–5, 7, 13; Shutterstock, pp. 6, 9, 12, 15, 19, 20, 26, 28–29; Wikimedia Commons, p. 11

Library of Congress Cataloging-in-Publication Data

Kenney, Karen Latchana, author.
  The science of roller coasters : understanding energy / by Karen Latchana Kenney.
    pages cm. -- (Science in action)
  Includes index.
  ISBN 978-1-62403-964-5
1. Roller coasters--Design and construction--Juvenile literature. 2. Force and energy--Juvenile literature. 3. Gravity--Juvenile literature. I. Title.
  GV1860.R64K46 2016
  791.06›8--dc23
                        2015026569

CONTENTS

THE SCREAM MACHINE!

It's finally your turn! You step into a roller coaster car and safety bars lock you in your seat. You hear the click, click, click, click as a machine pulls the cars up the first huge hill. Up at the very top, you see the steep drop ahead of you. Ready? Hang on tight!

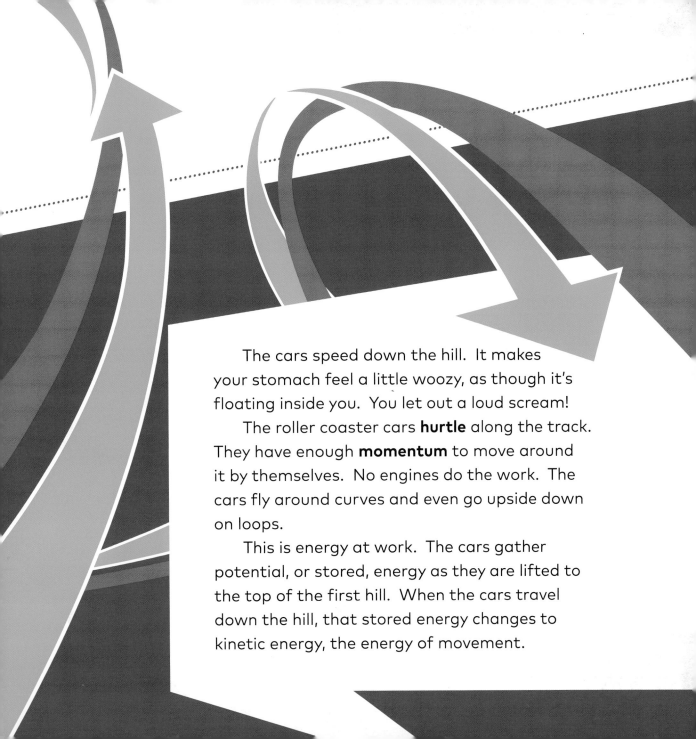

The cars speed down the hill. It makes your stomach feel a little woozy, as though it's floating inside you. You let out a loud scream!

The roller coaster cars **hurtle** along the track. They have enough **momentum** to move around it by themselves. No engines do the work. The cars fly around curves and even go upside down on loops.

This is energy at work. The cars gather potential, or stored, energy as they are lifted to the top of the first hill. When the cars travel down the hill, that stored energy changes to kinetic energy, the energy of movement.

WHAT IS ENERGY?

CHAPTER 1

Energy is the ability to do work, such as moving around a roller coaster track. There are many types of energy. Electrical, potential, and kinetic energy are three forms.

Motion is **essential** to energy. It can spark the change from one form to another. On most roller coasters, a machine uses electrical energy to pull cars up the first hill. That energy becomes potential energy, and then kinetic energy as the cars fly down the hill.

Energy constantly changes but is never destroyed. So, when one form of energy becomes another, the amount of energy is always the same. Forces play a role in this transformation.

The machine that pulls roller coaster cars up their first hill is an electric winch.

6

MEASURING ENERGY

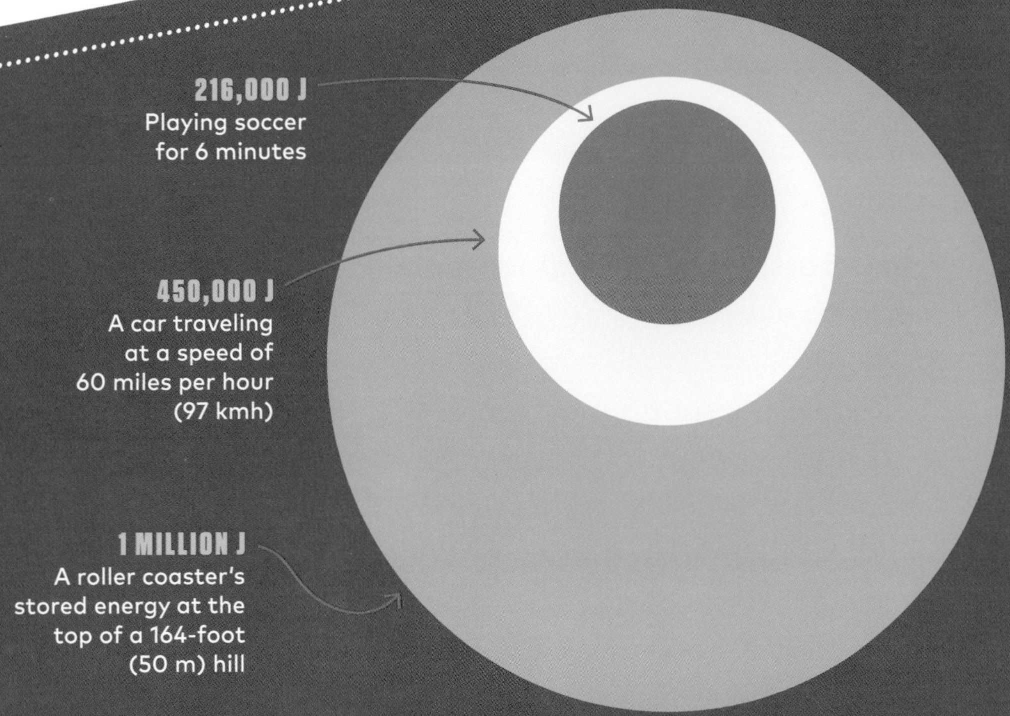

216,000 J
Playing soccer
for 6 minutes

450,000 J
A car traveling
at a speed of
60 miles per hour
(97 kmh)

1 MILLION J
A roller coaster's
stored energy at the
top of a 164-foot
(50 m) hill

Work equals the amount of force used times the distance an object is moved. The unit used to describe this work is a joule (J). This chart shows how many joules it takes to do different kinds of work.

GRAVITY AND
DESIGN

Roller coasters require a great amount of potential energy to work. How do roller coaster designers create this energy? The force of gravity plays a large role.

Remember that a machine pulls a roller coaster car up its first hill, creating potential energy. Then, the car crests the hill. As it does, gravity's pull causes the car to fall back toward the earth, creating kinetic energy.

In addition to pulling objects toward Earth's surface, gravity also pulls all matter together. Anything that has mass and takes up space has matter. The more matter an object has, the more gravitational pull it has on other objects.

Earth is a very large object. Its gravitational pull is very strong. This pull, along with gravitational potential energy, causes roller coaster cars to plummet down hills with amazing speed.

Gravity is at work as roller coaster cars dive down a supersteep drop.

HEIGHT AND ENERGY

As roller coaster cars race down toward Earth's surface, their stored energy is used in movement. Gravity turns the potential energy into kinetic energy.

Gravity also affects the amount of potential energy the cars store. When an object is above Earth's surface, it has gravitational potential energy. The higher it is above the surface, the more energy it stores.

At the very top of a hill, the cars have a great amount of gravitational potential energy. Once they tip over the hilltop, gravity kicks in. This force pulls the cars down the hill at top speed.

Roller coaster designers think about gravity's pull when designing roller coasters. Because a greater height creates greater potential energy, the first hill of a roller coaster is the highest hill of the track. At the bottom of the hill, the cars have the least amount of potential energy, but the greatest amount of kinetic energy.

LAMARCUS THOMPSON

American inventor LaMarcus Thompson was born in 1848. He loved designing and building things from a young age.

As an adult, Thompson rode on a former mining train. Miners once used it to move coal down a mountain. When Thompson rode it, the train was a tourist attraction. His ride sparked an idea to build a ride.

Thompson finished building his ride in 1884 at Coney Island, New York. He called it the Gravity Pleasure Switchback Railway. It was the first roller coaster in the United States.

LaMarcus Thompson's Gravity Pleasure Switchback Railway

The first hill is not the only hill on a roller coaster ride.
Roller coaster designers develop tracks that have high
and low points until the end. As the cars move along
these hills on the track, their energy changes back and
forth between potential and kinetic energy.

Remember that although energy changes, none
is ever lost. As energy changes forms during a

**It is often easy to spot the first hill of a roller coaster ride. It is
much taller than all other loops and hills!**

roller coaster ride, the total amount of energy stays the same.

Not all energy on a roller coaster becomes potential or kinetic energy, however. Some is converted into heat energy due to friction. Because of this, all hills must be lower than the first.

ROLLER COASTER ENERGY SHIFTS

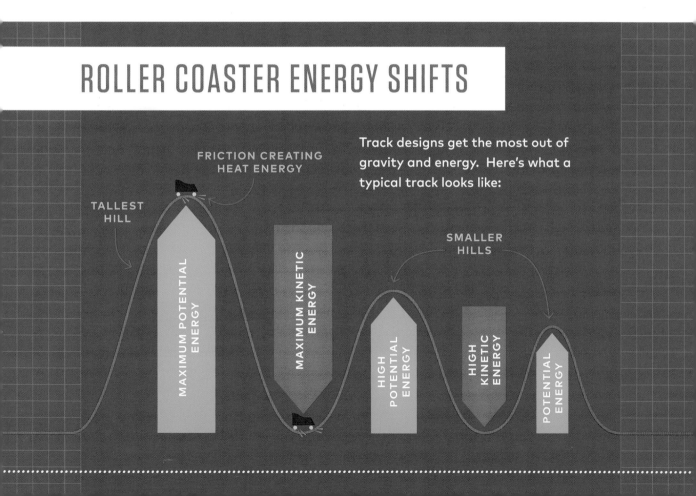

Track designs get the most out of gravity and energy. Here's what a typical track looks like:

FRICTION CREATING HEAT ENERGY

TALLEST HILL

SMALLER HILLS

MAXIMUM POTENTIAL ENERGY

MAXIMUM KINETIC ENERGY

HIGH POTENTIAL ENERGY

HIGH KINETIC ENERGY

POTENTIAL ENERGY

SUPERFAST SPEEDS

Zooming down hills, roller coaster cars can reach some pretty high speeds. Fast speeds are what thrill-seeking riders want in a good roller coaster. The world's fastest roller coaster is Formula Rossa. It is located in Abu Dhabi, United Arab Emirates. The ride goes as fast as 150 miles per hour (240 kmh)! The fastest roller coaster in the United States is Kingda Ka. It is in Jackson, New Jersey, and reaches 128 mph (206 kmh).

Riders scream aboard the Kingda Ka roller coaster.

Loops, coils, and turns are part of what make whizzing roller coaster rides exciting!

But roller coaster cars don't maintain these superfast speeds along the entire track. That is because they don't just travel in one direction. The cars move up and down. They screech around corners and make seemingly impossible loops.

An object moving at a certain speed in a certain direction has **velocity**. A roller coaster is always changing its velocity. The sudden switches in direction and speed are what make the ride full of surprises.

DIRECTION AND ACCELERATION

A roller coaster track's change in direction affects the roller coaster cars' speed. The cars slow down while climbing uphill. Then they **accelerate** quickly as they zoom from the top of a hill to its bottom. How fast the cars accelerate is key to a great ride. Going from slow to superfast can create quite a thrill!

The fastest roller coaster in the United States, the Kingda Ka, accelerates to its top speed in 3.5 seconds. But a Japanese roller coaster has the fastest acceleration in the world. It is the Dodonpa roller coaster in Fujiyoshida, Japan.

This Dodonpa uses jets and compressed air to launch its cars in motion. The cars accelerate from 0 to 107 miles per hour (172 kmh) in just 1.8 seconds! This track also has **hairpin** curves, another key feature in great roller coaster rides.

The Dodonpa roller coaster is known for being one of the
scariest coasters in the world!

TURNS
AND LOOPS

CHAPTER 4

Roller coasters take riders up, down, and around twisting tracks. Some roller coasters even turn riders upside down through loops! What keeps the cars on the track on these loops?

The shape of the loop is very important to keeping cars on roller coaster tracks. At first glance, a roller coaster loop might look as though it is a circle. But a circle shape is not safe.

While working to complete a loop, the cars lose **acceleration**. If they move too slowly, the cars could fall off the track at the top of the loop. To complete circular loops on roller coasters made in the past, the cars needed to enter the loop with **incredible** speed. This speed was too dangerous for passengers. So roller coaster designers today use a new, safer shape.

Riders move in an inverted turn when whizzing through a roller coaster's clothoid loop.

Modern roller coaster loops are a clothoid loop shape. It is similar to an upside-down water drop. The track curves more sharply at the top of a clothoid loop than at the top of a circle loop. This causes **acceleration** to increase. The forward force of acceleration is stronger than gravity's pull on the cars. This keeps cars safely on the track.

As your roller coaster car goes upside down in a loop, gravity's force pulls you toward Earth. Your shoulders strain against the safety harness. During other parts of the ride, your body is pushed down into your seat. When this occurs, another force is at work.

Centripetal force occurs along a curved path. It pushes out from the inside of the curve. It forces objects to move in a curved path rather than straight line.

Centripetal force is at work all over an amusement park. It is the force that keeps you pressed against the back of the car when you ride the Scrambler.

A banked turn tilting toward the inner part of a roller coaster track

Roller coasters have different types of turns. Turns where the track lies **horizontal** to the ground are flat turns. During a flat turn, riders feel pushed against one side of a car.

Banked turns have tracks that angle upward on the outside edge. When roller coaster cars take banked turns, they tilt toward the inner part of the turn. This angle causes **centripetal force** to push riders down into their seats.

FEELING G-FORCES

Some of the fun of a roller coaster is how weird it makes you feel. You get light-headed and feel dizzy. Your insides feel like they're floating around in your body. Some people feel **queasy**. Roller coaster rides also make people scream with excitement and even slight terror!

The trick for roller coaster designers is to make riders feel as though they are in danger, even though they are not. Designers often use the effects of g-forces to accomplish this.

Many people raise their arms when riding a roller coaster. This can increase the floating feeling g-forces create during the ride.

While g-forces can make you lightheaded on a roller coaster ride, its twists and turns can also make you dizzy!

A g-force is the effect on a person's body that is caused by quick **acceleration**. One g is equal to the force of gravity on Earth. A roller coaster's g-forces change throughout the ride.

At the bottom of a big hill, g-forces are strong. They can reach 4 to 5 g's for a few seconds. Blood rushes from the head to lower parts of the body, making riders feel light-headed. But these funny feelings and the roller coaster ride are over before you know it!

END OF THE RIDE

Some roller coaster rides take only take seconds to complete. The Kingda Ka travels 3,118 feet (950 m) in just 50.6 seconds! How do you get such a high-speed ride to stop? Friction and magnets!

Friction is a force that occurs between two objects. As two surfaces slide against each other, friction fights against the motion. Friction fights against the forward motion of roller coaster cars. It also transforms some of the ride's kinetic energy to heat.

Remember that during the ride, potential and kinetic energy switch forms in a constant back and forth. The portion of kinetic energy that becomes heat energy from friction leaves that loop. Nearer the end of the ride, the cars have less energy. The track's hills get smaller and smaller. Finally, it levels out. This helps the cars slow down.

Roller coasters have three types of wheels, all of which create friction. Guide wheels are the main wheels. Road wheels roll along the top of the track, and upstop wheels roll along beneath the track.

Special clamps also help slow the cars down. The clamps are located underneath roller coaster cars. They close around a beam at the ride's end. This creates additional friction that slows the cars.

Magnets also help with this task. A magnetic braking system sits by the track. It has magnets that pull toward each other. This force turns more of the cars' kinetic energy into heat energy. This heat energy moves through the braking system, helping bring the ride to an end.

FORCES AND FUN

A roller coaster ride is filled with terrifying dips, forceful turns, and fast **acceleration.** It feels scary and fun all at the same time! Riders also feel **intense** g-forces as they zoom along the ride. Their stomachs drop. They are flipped upside down, pushed through loops, and dropped down huge hills.

Potential energy builds as roller coaster cars move up hills. It converts to kinetic energy as gravity causes the cars to speed toward the ground.

Roller coaster cars fly through loops and take sharp corners. The cars'

What is your favorite roller coaster thrill? Do you like taking twisting turns? What about being flipped upside down?

26

Energy and forces create big fun on roller coasters. Riders are all smiles at the end!

velocity and **acceleration** change as they take these loops and turns. Friction and **centripetal forces** help keep cars on the track. At ride's end, friction and magnets bring the speeding cars to a stop.

Roller coasters make maximum use of energy and gravity. These forces allow the cars to take turns, twists, and loops at **incredible** speeds. They power the thrills and chills roller coaster riders love!

MINI MARBLE
COASTER

AN EXPERIMENT WITH ENERGY

QUESTION

Can you create energy transfer to make a marble travel along a mini roller coaster track?

RESEARCH

You have learned that roller coasters rely on energy and gravity to work. Can you design a mini track that builds potential energy that will then switch to kinetic energy? Here are materials you'll need to find out:

- foam tubing (found at hardware stores)
- scissors
- tape
- marble

PREDICT

What will happen when you drop a marble onto the track you create? What designs will allow it to **accelerate** and transfer energy successfully? Decide how your track should look. Then **predict** how the marble will travel along it.

TEST

1. Cut one or more pieces of tubing in half the long way. Then tape the pieces together to make a track.

2. Tape the tube track to walls, floors, and tables. Add hills and loops. Make sure the track starts at a high point and ends at a low point.

3. Let your marble go at the high point of the track. Does it lose energy as it goes? If so, adjust the track. Experiment to see what works best to power the marble to the end.

ASSESS

Did your marble successfully complete its ride? Did you correctly predict what design would work best? Did you have to make adjustments? Write down your results. Then change the track and experiment again!

GLOSSARY

accelerate – to move faster or gain speed.

centripetal force – the force that pulls toward the center of a circle on an object moving around that circle.

essential – very important or necessary.

hairpin – an extremely sharp, U-shaped turn.

horizontal – level with the horizon, or side to side.

hurtle – to move with great force and speed.

incredible – amazing or unbelievable.

intense – marked by great energy.

momentum – the force or strength objects have when moving.

predict – to guess something ahead of time on the basis of observation, experience, or reasoning.

queasy – having a sick feeling in the stomach, feeling as though one may throw up.

velocity – the speed of something in a given direction.

WEBSITES

To learn more about Science in Action, visit **booklinks.abdopublishing.com**. These links are routinely monitored and updated to provide the most current information available.

INDEX